Coconut's

Puzzle Book

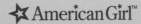
American Girl™

Editorial Development: Rick Walton, Elizabeth Chobanian,
Michelle Watkins

Art Direction: Camela Decaire, Chris Lorette David

Design: Camela Decaire

Production: Kendra Pulvermacher, Mindy Rappe, Cindy Hach

Illustrations: Casey Lukatz

Coconut's taking you for a walk through pages of puzzles. Our pup will lead the way through brain teasers, crazy crosswords, mixed-up mazes, and more. You'll wind through word searches and jump over riddles. Don't peek at the answers until you're done. Just remember—getting stuck is part of the fun!

Good luck!

Coconut's Crisscross

Fit into the crisscross grid these things you use when you take care of Coconut. The first two words are already done for you.

DOGHOUSE   MAT
SHAMPOO   WATER
TOWEL   DISH
TREATS   BALL
COLLAR   LEASH
WASHTUB   TOY
BRUSH   BONE
FOOD

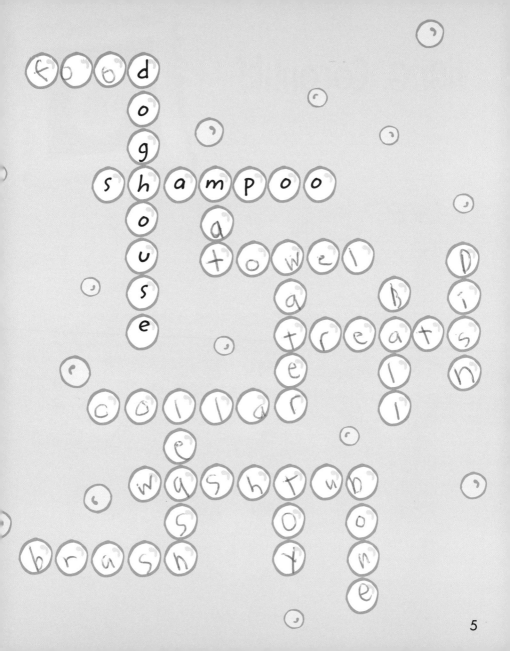

food
dog
g
shampoo
o
u   a
s   towel   D
e   a   B   i
treats   s
e   l   n
collar   l
e
washtub
s   o   o
brush   y   n
e

5

Here, Coconut!

Coconut is lost in a crowd of look-alikes. See if you can find her. Only one is the real Coconut and looks *exactly* like her picture.

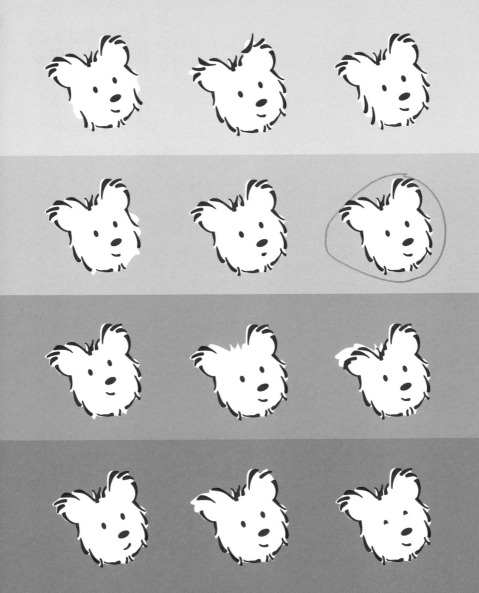

Two Together

Best friends go together like peanut butter and jelly.
Unscramble each of the words below to find other
perfect pairs.

UANT _aunt_ & UCLNE _uncle_

BAERD _Bread_ & BTUTRE _Butter_

SUGH _Hugs_ & KSISSE _Kisses_

HSOSE _Shoes_ & OSKSC _socks_

KAEC _Cake_ & CIE EMARC _Ice cream_

TLAS _Salt_ & RPPEPE _Pepper_

Come Here!

Try this out on a pal: Say to her, "Can you say 'Come
here, Coconut!' with your mouth closed?"

Then explain, "Sure you can! Just say, 'Come here,
Coconut, with your mouth closed.'"

Surf's Up!

Test your memory! Look at this picture for one minute. Then turn the page to see how much you can remember.

Hello from Hawaii

See how much you remember about the picture on page 9. Without looking back, fill in the blanks of the postcard below.

Hawaii's been great from the moment we boarded our cruise ship, called _Empress_. Coconut loves wearing her pretty _lea_. We rented gear, so we can learn how to _surf_ and _snorkel_. There are even _Dolphins_ swimming with us in the ocean! Everything's so beautiful! The beaches

are covered with _shells_ and _starfish_. The _Sun_ has been shining all day, and there are two _hot - air_ _balloons_ flying over our ship. We're going to ride in one tomorrow!

Coconut's Chase

Follow the lines to see where Coconut has chased each of her friends.

Bird   Butterfly   Frog   Grasshopper   Ladybug   Mouse

A Good Friend Is ...

When Coconut sniffs out a true friend,
she looks for someone who is:

CARING

FAIR

HELPFUL

LOVING

SINCERE

UNDERSTANDING

COMPASSIONATE

FRIENDLY

HONEST

LOYAL

THOUGHTFUL

CONSIDERATE

GENEROUS

KIND

PATIENT

TRUSTWORTHY

Find these words hidden forward, backward,
up, down, and diagonally.

```
I X U U M E V D C O G L E Z Z J I Y F G
R W W G S D X S N E T N Q R N A H D A E
I A X M N Q K E N R L E Q C E T E D I N
E T A N O I S S A P M O C K R C H C R E
F Q P U N T D L A C P C Y O Y E N C K R
F R C D G J K N Q Q K S W A L G Q I P O
X Q I X I L V W A Y F T F P L N E C S U
N B B E M S L G I T S K F C M I T D O S
I C X O N F P W R U S U O Z W R A O L X
S M O I I D G P R J L R F Y T A R H G K
V Z T H D K L T S F D J E H H C E V V O
T V Z Q X L B Y V K B Z D D S U D L E P
I J A K D K O A X T Z J Y H N P I H K U
D D Q D K H P J W V U T R I K U S G Y U
T H O U G H T F U L S P I Z I H N M Z V
T N E I T A P F P E L O Y Y A D O Y E U
Q B V X I D F G N L O V I N G A C V I O
I U H M P D F O I O X V R A F D M S C W
H N E K U A H B V M C K H X Y Z L Q E E
N A M I F U B A Z E V X V F M I X A W U
```

A Dark and Stormy Night

6

3

1

Number the pictures below so they're in the right order.

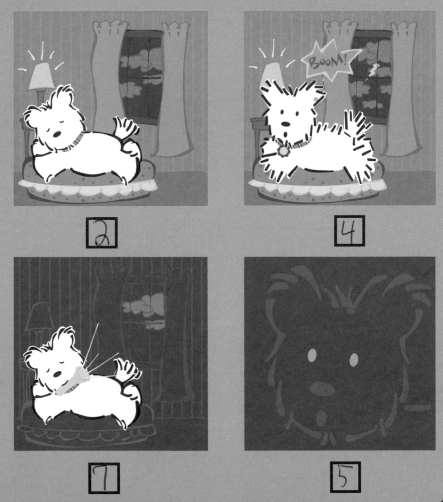

15

Run, Coco, Run!

Coconut ran a race with 39 other pups. All the ribbons have numbers on them except Coconut's. Can you figure out what place she came in? Write it on her ribbon!

Cuddly Coconut

Use the clues to fill in the blanks, then read the circled letters to see what Coconut wants you to give her.

Coconut likes to jump into your _(a)_ _r_ _m_ _s_
If it's not on your foot, Coconut will chew your _(h)_ _e_ _w_
Coconut cheers you up when you feel this color. _b_ _l_ _(u)_ _e_
Birds do this. Coconut likes when you do it, too. _s_ _i_ _n_ _(g)_

_a_ _hug_
(2 words)

Cheer Up, Little Pup!

If Coconut is discouraged, what should you do?
Use the code below to find the answer.

	0	1	2	3	4
5	A	F	K	P	U
6	B	G	L	Q	V
7	C	H	M	R	W
8	D	I	N	S	X/Y
9	E	J	O	T	Z

_g_ _i_ _v_ _e_   _h_ _e_ _r_   _a_
61 81 64 90   71 90 73   50

_p_ _u_ _p_   _t_ _a_ _l_ _k_.
53 54 53   93 50 62 52

18

Spell It Out

Using the definitions shown below, figure out the first three words. Next, put their letters in the right spaces to complete the sentence below.

A place to sleep $\dfrac{b}{1} \dfrac{e}{2} \dfrac{d}{10}$

Fish arms $\dfrac{f}{5} \dfrac{i}{7} \dfrac{n}{9} \dfrac{s}{11}$

What you should do if you're tired $\dfrac{r}{6} \dfrac{e}{8} \dfrac{s}{3} \dfrac{t}{4}$ ~~them~~

Coconut and I are

$\dfrac{b}{1} \dfrac{e}{2} \dfrac{s}{3} \dfrac{t}{4} \quad \dfrac{f}{5} \dfrac{r}{6} \dfrac{i}{7} \dfrac{e}{8} \dfrac{n}{9} \dfrac{d}{10} \dfrac{s}{11}!$

19

In the Bag!

The object of the game is to force your opponent to cross off the only sleeping bag with Coconut in it. To start, player 1 crosses out as many bags as she wants in any one row across. Player 2 can cross out more bags in the same row or choose another row. Players take turns until only the bag with Coconut remains. The player who must cross out this bag loses! Before you play, copy the page so you can play again.

Yum!

Fill in the blanks to complete each word. Hint: The missing letters follow one after another in the alphabet—like ABC or XYZ.

Shopping List

AVO C A D O e S

SPA G H ETT I

CA N TAL O U P E

_ _ _ RNO _ _ ER

BEA _ S _ U _

_ E _ O _ ADE

BRATWU R S t

S t u FFING

Hitting the Slopes!

Brrr! Time to put on your thinking cap. Concentrate on this picture for one minute. Then turn the page to test your memory.

Downhill Thrill

See how much you remember about the picture on page 23. Without looking back, fill in the blanks of the postcard below.

It's a good thing we're not afraid of heights! We're way up in the _mountain_, riding on a _chair lift_ to get to the top of our slope. From here you can see the entire village we're visiting. We counted _4_ ski runs. The weather is perfect! Right now it's _snow_ ing, so we should have a fresh slope to ski on!

Coconut looks great! Her skis are colored _pink_ with polka dots, and she has a matching _hat_ and _gogs_. What a stylish pup!

Wish us luck on the way down!

COC

B Friends

Can you figure out the words these friendly B's are in?
The hints will help you.

g o B B t l e — What Coconut heard a turkey say

b u B B l e s — What Coconut likes in her bath

r a B B i t — A furry animal Coconut likes to chase

d r i B B l e — What you can do with a basketball

r i B B o n — Something you wear in your hair

Coconut's Tricks

1. Coconut can breathe underwater. How can you help her?
2. Coconut can stick out her tongue and touch her ear.
   How does she do it?

1. Hold a glass of water over her head.

2. She sticks out her tongue and touches her ear with her paw.

2 for 1

Match each word with a word in a different circle. Put the words together to make a compound word.

bag
cake
earth
ground
wheel
straw

barrow
corn
egg
grass
quake
sun

berry
cracker
flower
pipe
pop
frog

bull
cup
fire
plant
hopper
play

1. bagpipe
2.
3.
4.
5.
6.
7.
8.
9.
10.
11.
12.

Coco on the Go

Use the letters in the words on the left to make a new word.
(Hint: The new word will be a place where you and a friend could go.)

each, ache, cab _____beach_____

elk, kale, leak _____

airy, briar, lab, rail, rib _____

me, moi, move, some, vise _____

emus, mums, muse, sue, sum _____

ark, pa, rap _____

around, dragon, play, pony _____

loop, lop, polo _____

ore, rest, rose, toes _____

Scrambled Leashes

Coconut wants to go for a walk. Can you figure out which hook her leash is hanging on so that you can take it off for her?

Ready, Set, O!

Start with a letter on the outside of the wheel. Add O. Then add another letter from the outside of the wheel to create a three-letter word. Example: WON. See if you can make 30 three-letter words!

_____   _____   _____

_____   _____   _____

_____   _____   _____

_____   _____   _____

_____   _____   _____

_____   _____   _____

_____   _____   _____

_____   _____   _____

_____   _____   _____

_____   _____   _____

31

Dog Dreams

Unscramble the words below to find out what Coconut likes to do.

1. krab _bark_
2. scharct _scratch_
3. cheas _chase_
4. aypl _play_
5. clik _lick_
6. keash _sheek_
7. klaw _walk_
8. eleps _sleep_

Coconut's Code

Use the key below to decipher this message.

Q: 2Y343 WY97OE 697 5QI3 D9D9H75 2Y3H WY3'W W8DI?

A: 59 Q E9T594.

Key:

Q	G	D	E	3	R	T	Y	8	U	I	O	J
A	B	C	D	E	F	G	H	I	J	K	L	M

H	9	0	1	4	W	5	7	F	2	S	6	A
N	O	P	Q	R	S	T	U	V	W	X	Y	Z

_____

_____

_____

_____

_____

Sticks and Squares

Coconut fetched these sticks and made them into nine squares. Can you take out eight of the sticks and leave two squares? Hint: Try using toothpicks to figure it out!

Catch!

You're throwing the ball for Coconut to fetch. You throw, and she brings it back. You throw; she brings it back. Then you throw the ball hard, but it comes right back on its own. How can this be?

You threw it straight up into the air!

Coconut Goes Wild!

How much can you remember about Coconut's safari?
Look at this picture for one minute. Then turn the page to test your memory.

Coco on Safari

See how much you remember about the picture on page 35. Without looking back, fill in the blanks of the postcard below.

A safari is a real adventure! Coconut is learning to ride an _____ ! There are cool animals everywhere! I saw a _____ as tall as the trees. There are _____ swinging from branches. And four _____ are just hanging out under the hot _____. Coconut has to wear a special _____ to keep cool. We flew here in a bright _____ plane. And I'm so excited, because tonight we're camping out in a _____ !

We'll write more tomorrow!

Happy Birthday, Coconut!

Friends share very special days. On Coconut's birthday, you and Coconut played games, sang songs, played with puzzles, quickly opened presents, hid in the boxes, and played with the wrapping paper.

In the paragraph above, you'll find every letter of the alphabet but one. Can you figure out which letter is missing?

Amazing Mazes

Don't be left waiting in the
wings! Fly from start to finish!

Start

Finish

Start

Coconut needs some treats!
Help her get to the pet store.

Finish

Word for Word

Make as many words as you can out of the letters in "Coconut." (Each letter can be used only once in each word.) When you're finished, fit the words into the grid.

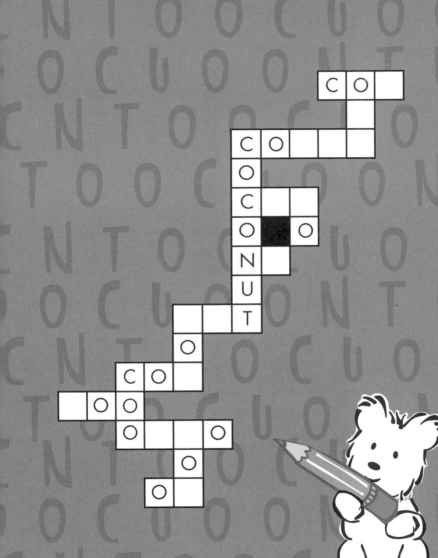

Daisy Chains

Fill in the blanks with words that make sense when they're combined with the words both before and after them.

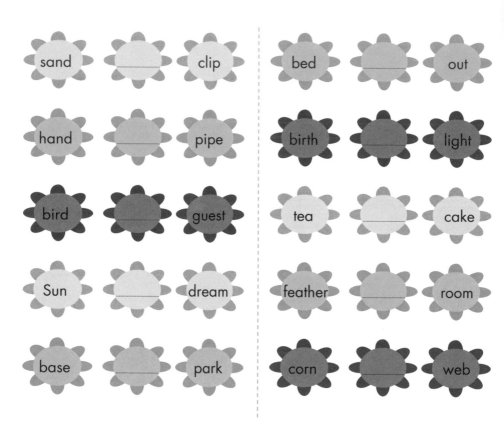

sand   _____   clip

hand   _____   pipe

bird   _____   guest

Sun   _____   dream

base   _____   park

bed   _____   out

birth   _____   light

tea   _____   cake

feather   _____   room

corn   _____   web

Math Maze

Each row is a math equation, reading from left to right and from top to bottom. Fill in the circle blanks with either a plus or a minus sign to make each equation work.

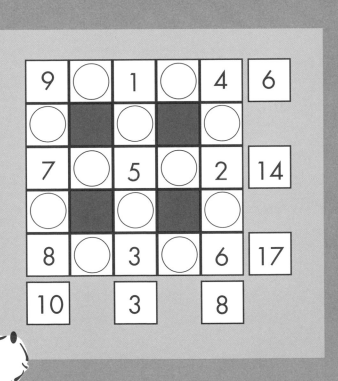

Take a Walk

Nothing gets Coconut's tail wagging like a walk around the block. Find all the things she sniffs and sees along the way.

BIRDS
CHILDREN
FIRE HYDRANT
HOUSES
SIDEWALK
TREES
BUSHES
DOGS

FLOWERS
LAKE
SQUIRRELS
BUTTERFLIES
FENCE
GRASS
PARK
STOP SIGNS

```
E K A L Q M S C H C L B X S H S T W P S
S Q U I R R E L S H D I E E O B C A S X
S R E W O L F Q E I X R I I A F R A H W
S T W X Z T M E A L M D Y L Z K R G B O
L G O D T V E R A D M S V F T G V D Y Q
Z P O P Y R X Z Q R K N P R V N E E V V
Y K Y D S D Z M O E E R F E X P I Z T U
O P S H O I P E S N S C X T S X D N Z Z
V M W Y G J G I Z K T P J T J F A A Q Y
Z L A H P R D N E M E V J U E R E R S S
C A S I Y E Q G S O U R Q B D I E N U K
R I T E W N O F Y V H F K Y H V W P C V
R J A A H J C N L L U T H V G V I N K E
D P L I F S B W N T B E D E T P H R U K
M K O X W U U S J V R S C P Q L E V R K
F A L N I W O B D I M E T R E E S N P K
R A B I H I A E F T E S Y H K Q M Y R N
C P K H G K P A G V F U Y L O I W G W O
Z U Y R A Q O N Q V F O B T E C Y S R S
Z C J N C D H Y N H V H K B D D Z V K Z
```

45

Critter Crossing

Coconut has lots of buddies in her backyard. Solve this crossword puzzle to find out who they are.

Across

2. Small rodent, rhymes with "house"
4. Slow-moving animal in a shell
6. Yellow and black insect that buzzes
8. Insect with colorful wings
9. Colorful beetle

Down

1. Small, striped rodent
3. Animal that has a bushy tail and likes nuts
5. Furry animal that likes Easter
7. Leaping animal similar to a toad
8. Feathered friend

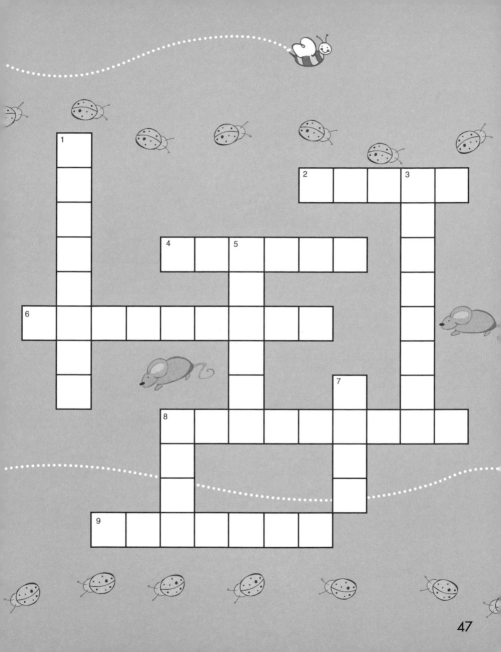

47

White and Fluffy

Unscramble the words below. (Hint: Each is a word for something fluffy and white.) Copy the letters in the numbered boxes to answer the question below.

OSNW ☐ ☐(5) ☐(2) ☐

OTCNTO ABLSL ☐(8) ☐ ☐ ☐(7) ☐   ☐ ☐(11) ☐ ☐ ☐

MOP MOSP ☐ ☐ ☐(12) – ☐ ☐(4) ☐ ☐

SOLCUD ☐(3) ☐ ☐ ☐(6) ☐ ☐

POSWLLI ☐(13) ☐ ☐ ☐ ☐ ☐ ☐

PEHSE ☐ ☐ ☐(10) ☐(15) ☐

PEIHPDW RCAME ☐ ☐ ☐(14) ☐ ☐ ☐ ☐   ☐(1) ☐(9) ☐ ☐ ☐

Coconut can't eat human treats, but if she could,
what would be her favorite dessert?

☐ ☐ ☐ ☐ ☐ ☐ ☐   ☐ ☐ ☐ ☐ ☐   ☐ ☐ ☐
1 2 3 4 5 6 7   8 9 10 11 12   13 14 15

48

Mix and Match

These letter tiles are mixed up! Unscramble them to reveal a message.

GIRL

'S B

EST

NUT

COCO

IS A

ND.

FRIE

hint!

'S B

From the Heart

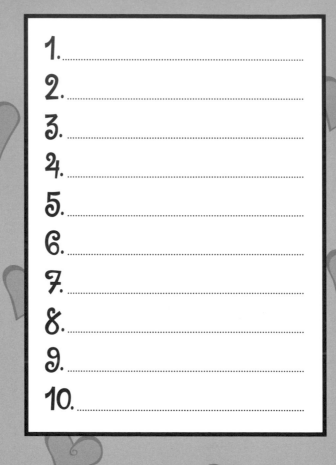

Quick! You have one minute to think of ten words that rhyme with heart. Go!

1. ....
2. ....
3. ....
4. ....
5. ....
6. ....
7. ....
8. ....
9. ....
10. ....

Crack the Code

Use the decoder to reveal one of Coconut's golden rules.

YOU CAN ALWAYS
15 11 3   13 10 6   10 18 19 10 15 22

COUNT ON A
13 11 3 6 12   11 6   10

GOOD FRIEND.
21 11 11 20   4 5 25 9 6 20.

Flower Power

Only two flower blossoms in Coconut's garden are exactly alike in color, size, and shape. See if you can find them.

Seeing Double

Fill in the blanks to complete each word. The first letter in each pair is the same as the second.

cu _ _ les   ho _ _ ow

ki _ _ es   c _ _ kies

gi _ _ les   parak _ _ t

squi _ _ les   ra _ _ oon

squi _ _ els   vac _ _ m

bu _ _ erflies   ru _ _ les

na _ _ ow   sw _ _ ts

fi _ _ le   snu _ _ le

l _ _ ps   ju _ _ le

bu _ _ les

ci _ _ amon

be _ _ s

tru _ _ les

su _ _ y

tr _ _ house

che _ _ y

f _ _ tball

dru _ _ er

cart _ _ ns

bumbleb _ _

a _ _ ordion

gr _ _ vy

ki _ _ y

raspbe _ _ y

ca _ _ ots

ball _ _ n

ch _ _ ry

Friend to Friend

There are lots of words for "friend." See if you can fit them into the crossword grid.

Across

SISTER
COMRADE
COMPANION
BUDDY

Down

AMIGA
MATE
PARTNER
FELLOW
PAL
CHUM

Answers

Coconut's Crisscross p. 4

f o o d
o
o
g
s h a m p o o
o   a
u   t o w e l   d
s   a   b   i
e   t r e a t s   s
      e   l   h
c o l l a r   l
      e
      w a s h t u b
      a   o   o
b r u s h   y   n
                   e

Two Together p. 8

aunt & uncle
bread & butter
hugs & kisses
shoes & socks
cake & ice cream
salt & pepper

Hello from Hawaii p. 10

Hawaii's been great from the moment we boarded our cruise ship, called Empress. Coconut loves wearing her pretty necklace (or lei). We rented gear, so we can learn how to surf and snorkel. There are even dolphins swimming with us in the ocean! Everything's so beautiful! The beaches are covered with shells and starfish. The sun has been shining all day, and there are two hot-air balloons flying over our ship. We're going to ride in one tomorrow!

Here, Coconut! p. 6

Coconut's Chase p. 11

bird—birdhouse;
butterfly—behind orange
flower; frog—under log;
grasshopper—on leaf;
ladybug—in grass;
mouse—behind rock!

A Good Friend Is ... p. 12

```
I X U U M E V D C O G L E Z Z J I Y F G
R W W G S D X S N E T N Q R N A H D A E
I A X M N Q K E N R L E Q C E T E D I N
E T A N Q I S S A P M O C K R C H C R E
F Q P U N T D L A C P C Y O Y E N C K R
F R C D G J K N Q Q K S W A L G Q I P O
X Q I X I L V W A Y F T F P L N E C S U
N B B E M S L G I T S K F C M I T D O S
I C X Q N F P W R U Q O Z W R A O L X
S M O I I D G P R J L R F Y T A R H G K
V Z T H D K L T S F D J E H H C E V V O
T V Z Q X L B Y V K B Z D S U D L E P
I J A K D K O A X T Z J Y H N P I H K U
D D Q D K H P J W V U T R I K U S G Y U
T H O U G H T F U L S P I Z I H N M Z V
T N E I T A P F P E L O Y Y A D O Y E U
Q B V X I D O G N L O V I N G A C V I O
I U H M P D F O I O X V R A F D M S C W
H N E K U A H B V M C K H X Y Z L Q E E
N A M I F U B A Z E V X V F M I X A W U
```

A Dark and Stormy Night p. 14

6, 3, 2, 4, 8, 1, 7, 5

Run, Coco, Run! p. 16
31

Cuddly Coconut p. 18
arms, shoe, blue, sing
a hug

Cheer Up, Little Pup!
p. 18
Give her a pup talk.

Spell It Out p. 19
bed, fins, rest
best friends.

Yum! p. 22
avocadoes
spaghetti
cantaloupe
turnover
bean soup
lemonade
bratwurst
stuffing

59

Downhill Thrill p. 24

It's a good thing we're not afraid of heights! We're way up in the mountains, riding on a ski lift to get to the top of our slope. From here you can see the entire village we're visiting. We counted 3 ski runs. The weather is perfect! Right now it's snowing, so we should have a fresh slope to ski on! Coconut looks great! Her skis are colored pink with polka dots, and she has a matching mask and hat. What a stylish pup! Wish us luck on the way down!

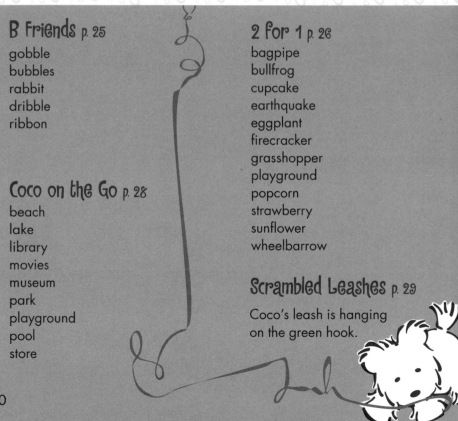

B Friends p. 25

gobble
bubbles
rabbit
dribble
ribbon

Coco on the Go p. 28

beach
lake
library
movies
museum
park
playground
pool
store

2 for 1 p. 26

bagpipe
bullfrog
cupcake
earthquake
eggplant
firecracker
grasshopper
playground
popcorn
strawberry
sunflower
wheelbarrow

Scrambled Leashes p. 29

Coco's leash is hanging on the green hook.

Ready, Set, O! p. 30

We found these possible answers. Did you find more?

bog	job	rot
bop	jog	row
bow	lop	rob
boy	lot	soy
got	low	sob
gob	lob	son
hop	log	tow
hot	nor	toy
how	not	tog
hog	now	ton
jot	pot	top
joy	pow	won

Dog Dreams p. 32

bark	lick
scratch	shake
chase	walk
play	sleep

Coconut's Code p. 33

Q: Where should you take Coconut when she's sick?
A: To a dogtor.

Sticks and Squares p. 34

Coco on Safari p. 36

A safari is a real adventure! Coconut is learning to ride an elephant! There are cool animals everywhere! I saw a giraffe as tall as the trees. There are monkeys swinging from branches. And four lions are just hanging out under the hot sun. Coconut has to wear a special hat to keep cool. We flew here in a bright red plane. And I'm so excited, because tonight we're camping out in a tent! We'll write more tomorrow!

Happy Birthday, Coconut! p. 37

The letter J is missing.

Amazing Mazes p. 38

Word for Word p. 40

Daisy Chains p. 42

sand	paper	clip
hand	bag	pipe
bird	house	guest
Sun	day	dream
base	ball	park

bed	time	out
birth	day	light
tea	cup	cake
feather	bed	room
corn	cob	web

Math Maze p. 23

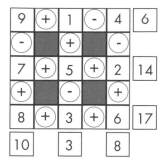

9	+	1	-	4	6
-		+		-	
7	+	5	+	2	14
+		-		+	
8	+	3	+	6	17
10		3		8	

Take a Walk p. 24

```
E K A L Q M S C H C L B X S H S T W P S
S Q U I R R E L S H D I E E O B C A S X
S R E W O L F Q E I X R I I A F R A H W
S T W X Z T M E A L M D Y L Z K R G B O
L G O D T V E R A D M S V F T G V D Y Q
Z P O P Y R X Z Q R K N P R V N E E V V
Y K Y D S D Z M O E E R F E X P I Z T U
O P S H O I P E S N S C X T S X D N Z Z
V M W Y G J G I Z K T P J T J F A A Q Y
Z L A H P R D N E M E V J U E R E R S S
C A S I Y E Q G S O U R Q B D I E N U K
R I T E W N O F Y V H F K Y H V W P C V
R J A A H J C N L L U T H V G V I N K E
D P L I F S B W N T B E D E T P H R U K
M K O X W U U S J V R S C P Q L E V R K
F A L N I W O B D I M E T R E E S N P K
R A B I H I A E F T E S Y H K Q M Y R N
C P K H G K P A G V F U Y L O I W G W O
Z U Y R A Q O N Q V F O B T E C Y S R S
Z C J N C D H Y N H V H K B D D Z V K Z
```

Critter Crossing p. 26

```
C
H         M O U S E
I                 Q
P    T U R T L E  U
M    A           I
B U M B L E B E E R
N    B           R
K    I        F  E
     B U T T E R F L Y
   B I        O
   I R        G
   L A D Y B U G
```

White and Fluffy p. 48

snow
cotton balls
pom-poms
clouds
pillows
sheep
whipped cream

Favorite Dessert:
COCONUT CREAM PIE

Mix and Match p. 49
Coconut is a girl's best friend.

From the Heart p. 50
art, cart, mart, start, depart, chart, part, tart, dart, smart (and you may find more!)

Crack the Code p. 51
You can always count on a good friend.

Flower Power p. 52

Seeing Double p. 54

cuddles	hollow	bubbles	cartoons
kisses	cookies	cinnamon	bumblebee
giggles	parakeet	bells	accordion
squiggles	raccoon	truffles	groovy
squirrels	vacuum	sunny	kitty
butterflies	ruffles	treehouse	raspberry
narrow	sweets	cherry	carrots
fiddle	snuggle	football	balloon
loops	juggle	drummer	cheery

Friend to Friend p. 56

The End

64